CAT'S REVENGE

More Than 101 Uses for Dead People

Produced by Philip Lief

A **WALLABY** BOOK

Published by Simon & Schuster

NEW YORK

This book is dedicated to cats and cat fanciers everywhere—to all the fans of Garfield, Kliban, Heathcliff, Morris, and Hodge who have been shocked and outraged by the appearance of two clearly ailurophobic titles on the bestseller list: THE OFFICIAL I HATE CATS BOOK and 101 USES FOR A DEAD CAT.

My cat and I were among the millions who greeted this event with a prolonged hiss. But when our fury had become a fur-ball less fierce, we started thinking. We remembered the saying, "Don't get mad—get even!" and began to plan a counter-attack.

What would *we* like to do with some of those cat haters out there? Well, my cat had plenty of ideas, I had a number myself, and so did other cats and their friends. Almost before we knew it, we had enough ideas to fill an entire book.

Cat haters, beware! THE CAT'S REVENGE is here!

Philip Lief

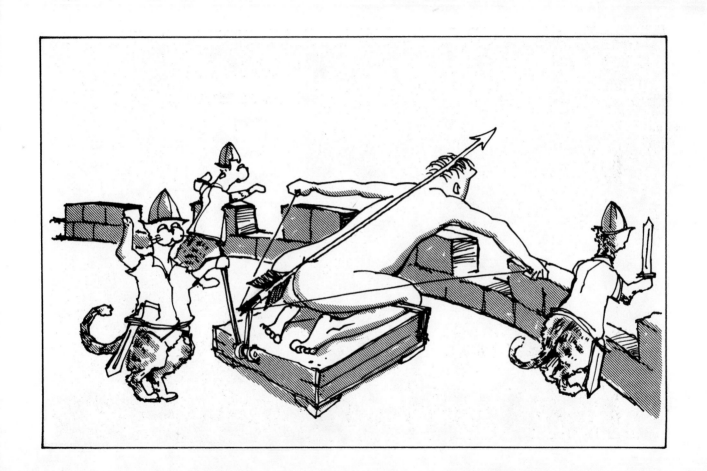

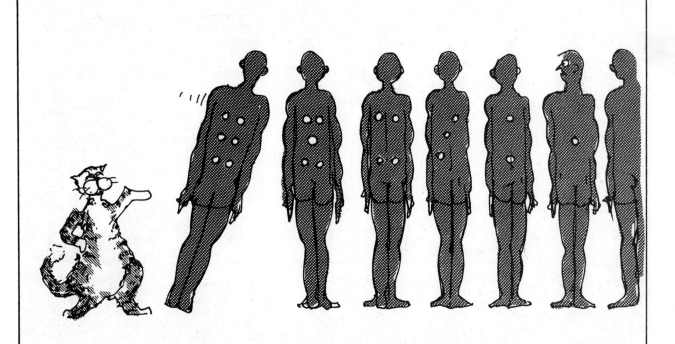

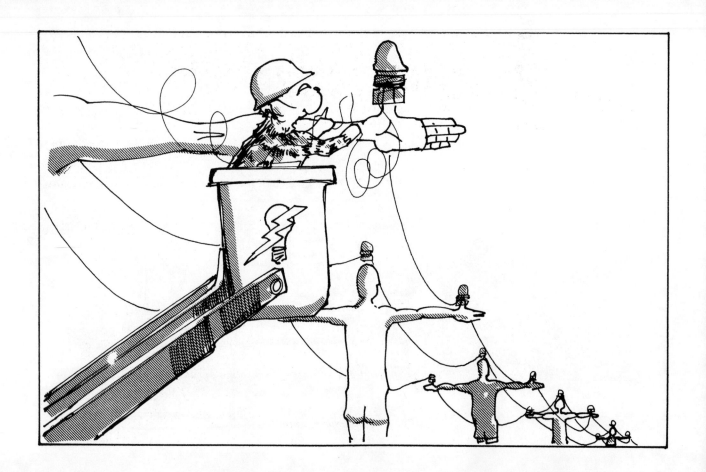

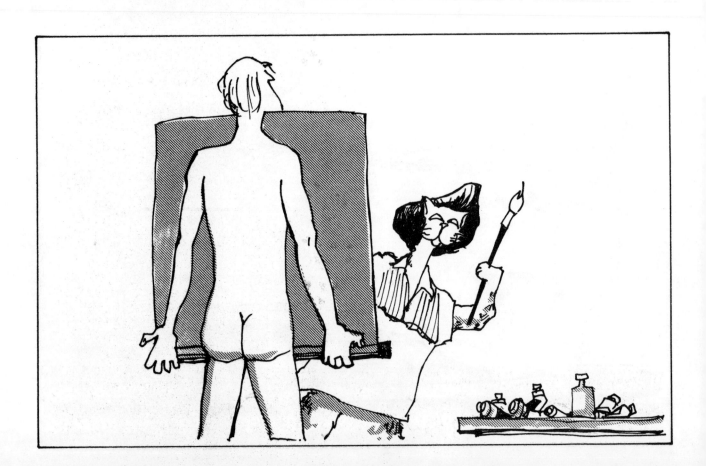

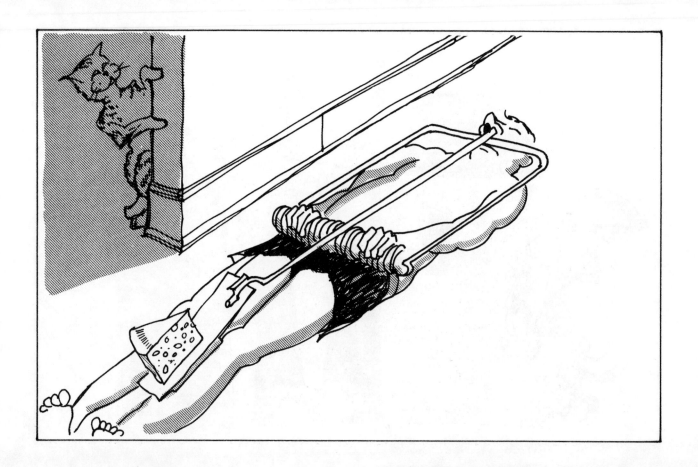